Integrated Mathematics 1

Project Book

The Project Book includes a project description, teaching commentary, a listing of the Working on the Unit Project exercises and the Completing the Unit Project exercises from the student textbook, a scoring rubric, a list of alternative projects from the student textbook, and a list of outside resources for each unit project in the student textbook.

McDougal Littell/Houghton Mifflin

Evanston, Illinois

Boston   Dallas   Phoenix

Acknowledgment
The authors want to thank Judith Collison, Research Associate, Technical Education Research Center, Cambridge, Massachusetts, for her contributions to this Project Book.

ISBN: 0-395-69813-8

23456789 - BW - 98 97 96 95

Contents

Assessing Student Performance on the Unit Projects

Introduction

The Unit Projects in *Integrated Mathematics 1* involve students in cooperative tasks that include doing research, design work, reasoning, and the use of mathematical concepts. These tasks are open-ended and students' performance on them can be assessed only by a scoring scale that takes into account the nature of the tasks and the project goals themselves.

The goals of assessment also need to coincide with the goals of instruction. Since instructional goals can vary from school to school, and indeed from classroom to classroom, the scoring scale presented below should be interpreted as providing a broad and flexible framework for thinking about student performance on the unit projects. In fact, there are many ways to assess student performance on open-ended projects, and the one presented is just one possible approach that can be used or adapted to meet the needs of specific situations.

Scoring Scale

4 points   The student fully achieves all mathematical and project goals. The presentation demonstrates clear thinking and explanation.

3 points   The student substantially achieves the mathematical and project goals. The main thrust of the project and the mathematics behind it is understood, but there may be some minor misunderstanding of content, errors in computation, or weakness in presentation.

2 points   The student partially achieves the mathematical and project goals. A limited grasp of the main mathematical ideas or project requirements is demonstrated. Some of the work may be incomplete, misdirected, or unclear.

1 point   The student makes little progress toward accomplishing the goals of the project because of lack of understanding or lack of effort.

Project Goals

The scoring scale can be used to assess student performance on the project goals. Each of the ten unit projects in the textbook has goals that can be organized by the following categories and evaluated according to the 4-step scale.

Scoring Rubrics	Level of Complexity (Breadth) 1 2 3 4	Level of Difficulty (Depth) 1 2 3 4	Level of Under- standing 1 2 3 4	Mathematical Connections 1 2 3 4	Real-world Applications 1 2 3 4	Creativity 1 2 3 4
Mathematical Content: *Representations:* • variables • graphs • diagrams *Skills and Techniques:* • numerical operations • measurements *Concepts:* • functions • equalities • inequalities						
Reasoning: • brainstorming • deduction • use of patterns • problem solving						
Research: • design • use of statistics • interpreting data						
Presentation: • design • written report • oral report						
Technology: • use of calculators and computers						

Definition of Terms

Scoring Rubrics: These are aspects of the work done on the various projects. Not all will be applicable to all projects, and there may be some that are not represented here.

Level of Complexity: Considers the diversity of tasks involved in the project. For example, the extent of brainstorming or the breadth of research is taken into account.

Level of Difficulty: Considers the challenges involved in the project. Is the work easy to do or is it very demanding?

Level of Understanding: What evidence do students show in communicating and using mathematical ideas clearly?

Mathematical Connections: To what extent do students build on or extend prior mathematical knowledge by using new ideas arising from the project?

Real-world Applications: Is the student capable of recognizing and using mathematical ideas outside the classroom? Does the student have a greater understanding of the real world because of doing the project?

Creativity: Has the student approached the project in an original way or demonstrated a unique solution to it?

Working Together

The goals of having students work together in cooperative groups can be assessed separately from those of the other project goals. These goals are related to how well students in a group divide up the work of the project and actually carry out their tasks.

The 4-step rating scale can be used to rate the work of the group as a whole as well as to rate the performance of each individual student in the group.

Performance of the Group as a Whole

Collaborative Process: How well the group functions as a whole may be rated by the members of the group and by the teacher. Student participation in scoring gives group members a meaningful opportunity to reflect on the quality of their overall interaction.

Joint Presentations: The quality of these presentations may be assessed by the whole class, in voting for the best ones, or by rank ordering them. The presentations themselves also may be assessed using the criteria in the scoring matrix.

Arriving at or Developing Mathematical Content: The scoring of this should be done by the teacher, according to the criteria for successful completion of the project.

Unit 1 Project
Design a Logo

Project Description

- The goal of this project is to have students create a team logo that can be used to identify their math class. Students learn that various images from the unit can be used to design the logo.

  When designing a logo, students choose various shapes, patterns, symbols, numbers or terms and describe the reasons why each of these elements is part of the logo. To begin, students should describe what materials they need to use and where they can find them. A series of exercises throughout the unit will guide students as they work on their logo.

Teaching Commentary

This project helps to develop the mathematical intuition of students. They are engaged in creating an abstract representation (the logo) by relating and connecting the meanings of mathematical ideas. Students gain hands-on experience with symbols and learn how to connect symbolic representations to a real-world application.

Before the groups begin: It is important that students understand what a logo is and the purpose it serves. Analogical reasoning is used in creating a link between an idea and its representation. A whole-class discussion of topics should clear up any misconceptions.

Give students the opportunity to do research outside of class as individuals (perhaps as homework) to generate a list of logos in their environment. Students can then discuss ideas for the group logo in class. They can also discuss how they can contribute to the project. Group activities are more successful if all students make a contribution to the process and have a personal investment in the group's success.

Cooperative work: In small groups, students can consider each other's ideas, generate more ideas, discuss the meaning of a symbol, and divide the work within the group, taking into consideration each other's talents and preferences.

Connections: This project can be used to introduce the idea of a variable as a symbol and to explore the idea that concept maps represent and summarize relationships among ideas in much the same way that logos do. An understanding of the general use of symbols can facilitate an understanding of how specific symbols, such as numbers, operations, and relationships, are used in mathematics.

An interesting question that may be explored is whether there are benefits as well as drawbacks to immediate symbol recognition. For example, recognition of a flag, trademark, symbolic color, or logo can identify a person as either friend or foe. A discussion of this shows a link between ideas in mathematics and ideas in a social context. An interesting question for discussion is: Are logos like slogans? Other interdisciplinary connections are also natural here. The use of shorthand, musical themes in films or TV, buttons (political or other types), and family crests are some examples of analogous ideas outside of mathematics.

Creating a team handshake or a group rhythmic pattern captures the same idea as designing a logo and may make an understanding of the nature of symbols easier for those students who learn better using different approaches.

Working on the Unit Project Exercises

Section 1-1

37. Find some symbols without words that are understood internationally. Sketch three examples.

Section 1-2

47. To begin to think about a logo for your math class, list some words that you think of when someone says "mathematics."

Section 1-3

45. **a.** Your knowledge of mathematics will be growing this year. Look through this book for ideas about what you will be learning.

    b. Think about including in your logo a pattern of numbers or geometric shapes that suggest growth.

    c. Sketch one of your ideas.

Section 1-4

42. Magazines, newspapers, and telephone yellow pages are good places to find logos.

    a. Trace or cut out five different logos. Tape each logo to a separate piece of paper.

    b. Draw arrows to point out features of the logos that you think convey meaning about the product or service.

    c. Do the same with one of your sketches for your math logo.

Section 1-5

41. Find three different logos for the same kind of product, company, or organization. How are the logos alike? How are they different?

Section 1-6

32. Find a logo that includes congruent pieces. Describe the slides, turns, or flips that show the pieces are congruent. Why do you think congruent pieces are used in the logo?

Section 1-7

36. Find some logos that have symmetry and others that do not. Why do some companies use symmetry in their logos?

Completing the Unit Project

- Now you are ready to make your book cover. Your group can work together to make one cover to display or three individual versions of your group's logo design.
- On the inside flap of your book cover, explain what the patterns, symbols, numbers and shapes in your logo represent. Tell why you think your design identifies your math class.
- You may want to make an enlargement of your logo to display on a poster in your classroom. You may decide to make a bookmark showing a smaller version of your logo.

Look Back

Think about how your group worked together in the project. What recommendations would you give to a group of students just starting to work on this project to make their teamwork or their results better?

Assessing the Unit Project

4 points The logo design on the book cover uses patterns, symbols, numbers, and shapes in a way that is mathematically accurate. The written description and explanation for each element of the design are accurate and thorough. Reasons why this design identifies the math class are insightful. The logo is visually clear and appealing and may also be enlarged for use on a poster or reduced for use on a bookmark.

3 points The logo design on the book cover uses the mathematics adequately. The written description and explanation of the design elements is not as thorough as it could be. The visual effect of the logo is not entirely clear.

2 points The logo design on the book cover uses the mathematical elements in an incomplete or somewhat confusing manner. The description of each element of the design is incomplete. The reasons describing why this design identifies the math class are lacking or need more elaboration. This project should be returned with suggestions for improvements and a new deadline.

1 point This project cannot be evaluated. It is illegible, incomplete, or not understandable. The design should be returned with a new deadline for completion. The group should be encouraged to speak with the teacher as soon as possible.

Alternative Projects

Project 1: The Fibonacci Sequence

The list of numbers 1, 1, 2, 3, 5, 8, 13, 21, … is called the *Fibonacci sequence*. Describe this number pattern. Research the Fibonacci sequence and write a report about it. Describe how this pattern is displayed in nature.

Project 2: Create a Polygon Pattern

Regular polygons are shapes that have equal sides and equal angles. The triangle, square, and hexagon shown are regular polygons. Create a few patterns using these shapes. What kinds of patterns can you build with one kind type of polygon? with two types? with all three types? Sketch the patterns you make. Describe the symmetry of each design. Shade the polygons with different colors. How can the use of color affect the symmetry of your design?

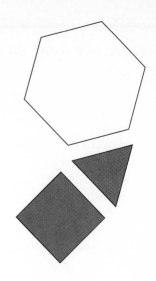

Outside Resources

Seymour, Dale and Reuben Schadler. *Creative Constructions*. Palo Alto, CA: Creative Publications, 1974.

Boles, Martha and Rochelle Newman. *Universal Patterns*. Bradford, MA: Pythagorean Press, 1990.

Dreyfuss, Henry. *Symbol Sourcebook: An Authoritative Guide to International Graphic Symbols*. New York: Van Nostrand Reinhold, 1984.

Unit 2 Project
Theme Poster Contest

Project Description

- The goal of this project is to have students create a theme poster that presents interesting numerical facts in ways that make them easier to understand.
- When making the poster, students present four numerical facts with four questions that can be answered using these facts, and an equation that can be solved to find another interesting fact. To begin, students can create an evaluation sheet that can be used to rate how well the posters incorporate various factors such as interest level, humor, creativity, or how well the posters help people understand the facts on display. A series of exercises throughout the unit will guide students as they work on their poster.

Teaching Commentary

The focus of this project is on the development of students' intuitive understanding of magnitude. In a way, this project is an extension of creating a logo in Unit 1, but the ideas represented are more complex. Correspondingly, the representation is also more complex. Posters are more extensive than logos, but they have many of the same characteristics. Analogical reasoning is used again by students as they create a two- or three-dimensional representation of a mathematical idea or relationship.

Some interesting, connecting topics of discussion are: How is creating a poster similar to creating a logo? What are posters used for? With the spread of electronic communications, how do you think the role of posters to present ideas will change?

Before the groups begin: Students should understand (1) the concept of *units* of measurement; (2) the way measurements are used in everyday life; and (3) the way the language of measurement is used to communicate. For example, in saying that you have heard something *a million times* or saying that you have been waiting to get into the theater *forever*, the language of measurement is being used.

Cooperative work: In a whole-class discussion, students can develop a set of criteria for judging the posters. Before joining a group, each student needs to think of number facts the group can use on its poster. Students should also think of criteria for evaluating the quality of the posters. Based on the individual suggestions of group members, the group can choose the facts, questions, and equation for the poster. The members of the group should decide how to divide up the work and then carry out the project. The *jigsaw method* of cooperation may be very useful for this project. If each group has "experts" with clearly defined roles, such as the *artist* or *layout specialist*, the experts can meet as a group to discuss ideas, problems, and solutions. As a preliminary exercise to the judging of the posters, it may be helpful to rotate the designs to other groups to see if they can guess what each poster represents. If the representations are too vague, groups should have a chance to use any suggestions to revise their posters.

Connections: A clear concept of magnitude is important to understanding positive and negative numbers, roots, powers and exponents, and to make sense of answers generated by calculators and computers. Some natural interdisciplinary extensions of this topic are understanding distances on Earth and in space, understanding time-zones, longevity, doses of medication, schedules, timetables, and historical time lines.

Working on the Unit Project Exercises

Section 2-1

42. *Research* Look in books, magazines, and newspapers for interesting numerical facts about the topic you choose for your theme poster. Write down at least 10 facts. Be sure to include counts, measurements, and percents.

Section 2-2

63. *Group Activity* Share the facts you have collected with your group. Do your facts include a negative number? If not, discuss whether one can reasonably be found in a fact about your theme. Plan to include a negative number on your poster if you can.

Section 2-3

55. a. *Group Activity* Check your group's facts. Is any number so large that you should write it in scientific notation? Is any number so small that it has a negative exponent when written in scientific notation? If not, brainstorm some facts about your theme that would include very large or very small numbers.

    b. *Research* Have each person in the group research one of the facts. Write the number in decimal notation and in scientific notation.

Section 2-4

29. Decide on an interesting way to help people understand the magnitude of each of your numerical facts except for the percent. You may want to compare a length or an area with something in your school.

Section 2-5

40. Some of your numerical facts are percents. Choose one to show in a circle graph. Tell what the whole circle represents, and tell the measure of the central angle you are using for your percent.

Section 2-6

39. *Group Activity* Show your group the circle graph you made for Exercise 40 in Section 2-5. Discuss your ideas for expressing your other numerical facts. Agree on at least four facts to illustrate on your theme poster. Include a very large number and a very small number in scientific notation, a measurement, and a percent.

Section 2-7

37. *Writing* Write four mathematical questions that can be answered using the facts included on your display. Write one question for each fact.

Section 2-8

32. **a.** You should still have some numerical facts that are not yet included on your theme poster. Write an equation that someone else could solve to find one of these numerical facts. For example, to find the number of legs on a butterfly, solve the equation $5x - 11 = 19$.

    b. Solve the equation you wrote in part (a) to be sure the solution matches the fact.

Section 2-9

55. Choose one of the facts going on your theme poster that could be expressed as an area. Suppose you express the fact as the area of a square. What would be the length of a side of the square?

56. Choose one of the four facts for your theme poster that could be expressed as a volume. Suppose you express the fact as the volume of a cube. What would be the length of an edge of the cube?

57. Compare the area and volume you chose in Exercises 55 and 56 with some areas and volumes that you know, such as the area of the United States or the volume of your school. Plan to include these comparisons on your theme poster.

Completing the Unit Project

Now you are ready to make your theme poster. Keep in mind how the poster will be judged as you make your display.

- Show at least four facts including a count, a measurement, and a percent. One number should be very large and one very small.
- For each fact write on question that can be answered using the information on your poster.
- Write an equation that can be solved to find another fact.

Be sure to include these details.

- Use a circle graph to illustrate the percent.
- Express your very large and very small numbers in decimal notation and in scientific notation.
- Describe at least one fact in terms of area or volume.

Look Back

What did you learn from this project that will help you make
sense of numbers that you read and hear about in everyday life?

Assessing the Unit Project

4 points The theme poster includes a counting fact, a measurement
fact, a percent fact, and either a very large or a very small
number. The questions are well written and use the
information on the poster. Complete solutions are
provided and the poster is visually appealing and clearly
relates to a theme.

3 points The theme poster is adequate. Not all the facts are
presented in an interesting way. The equations written
may not lead to another interesting fact. The poster's
theme does not relate clearly enough to the understanding
of magnitude.

2 points The theme poster is incomplete. The facts or details are
incomplete. The questions are only minimally acceptable.
This project should be returned with suggestions for
improvements and a new deadline.

1 point This theme poster cannot be evaluated. It is illegible,
incomplete, or not understandable. The project should be
returned with a new deadline for completion. The group
should speak with the teacher as soon as possible to
discuss the purpose and the format of the assignment.

Alternative Projects

Project 1: Redesigning a Room

Make plans to redesign a classroom in your school to make it more
efficient or more attractive. Plan an arrangement of desks and
workstations. Estimate how many desks will fit in the redesigned room.
Write a paragraph giving your reasons for redesigning the room. Explain
why your design is an improvement.

Project 2: Conducting an Interview

Numerals, fractions, and decimals are sometimes written differently in
other countries. Research some of the differences. Interview people who
have been to other countries to find out if they noticed any other ways
numbers are written. Report your findings to your class.

Outside Resources

Powers of Ten. Films of Charles and Ray Eames, Volume 1, 1982.
(video book)

The Challenge of the Unknown, "Comedy of Errors: The Sandwich."
Phillips Petroleum, 1986. Available from Karol Media, 3101 Geospace
Drive, Independence, MO 64056-1700. (free video and accompanying
book)

Unit 3 Project
Plan a Music Store

Project Description

- **The goal of this project is to have students collect data and use it to develop a business brochure that presents a plan for a new music store.**

  Before creating the brochure, students research the musical tastes and the buying habits of potential customers. They can begin by deciding on a name for the store and discuss where to look for the information they need about the musical tastes of potential customers. A series of exercises throughout the unit will guide students as they work on their brochure.

Teaching Commentary

This project focuses on a real-world application of mathematical skills and processes. In a sense, it is an extension of the poster project and involves the idea of creating a business brochure based upon the use of data collected by students.

The types of reasoning involved in this project are inductive and statistical. Students need to formulate questions, form and test hypotheses, and make reasoned predictions. They also must be able to understand, analyze, organize, and evaluate statistical data. The scope and limitations of the use of statistics can be discussed.

Before the groups begin: Working with all students, you may want to do a demographic description of your community, considering factors such as population size, cultural background, and mean and median age. The class can predict tastes and preferences and then design a study for testing their predictions. If possible, teach students how to use a computer spreadsheet, how to create a data base, and how to write a good questionnaire. Be sure they are familiar with the various graphic representations of data.

Cooperative work: This project should be done by small groups, each of which does the market research, design, and business brochure. An alternative way of proceeding is to work on one brochure produced by the entire class. The small groups would be assigned parts of the task in one of two ways: (1) all groups would be required to do part of the work involved and then bring the data together, or (2) each group would be assigned a different aspect of the project. For example, one group could design a questionnaire, another collect data, while others do library research, layout, editing, or graphics. The interdependence of all groups would promote a sense of community and responsibility to each other. This second approach can address a variety of learning styles.

Connections: A practical follow-up to the market research would be very useful in bringing real-life meaning to the project. Students could organize a tape/record sale as a fund raiser for scholarships, thus creating a temporary but real music store. Analysis of the sales would be a real-world test of the validity of students' theoretical conclusions.

Working on the Unit Project Exercises

Section 3-1

31. **a.** *Research* Follow the popularity of a song or a group using data from the last several months. You may want to use magazines such as *Billboard, Entertainment Weekly,* and *Variety.*

    b. Choose a format to display the data you collected.

    c. *Writing* Describe any trends you notice in the data you collected.

Section 3-2

35. **a.** *Research* Find the prices of at least 25 different recordings. Keep track of the type of music (for example, rock, classical, country) and the format of each recording (for example, cassette, CD, LP).

    b. Find the mean, the median, and the mode of all the price data.

    c. Find the mean, the median, and the mode of the prices of each of the different types of music. Which type has the largest mean?

    d. Find the mean, the median, and the mode of the prices of each of the different musical formats. Which format has the largest mean?

36. Suppose you ask 25 people to name their favorite type of music. Could you find the *mean*, the *median*, or the *mode* of their answers? Explain.

Section 3-3

28. *Research* Find the prices of seven different recordings. Make a line plot of the prices. Write an inequality to describe the shortest interval of the number line that contains all the prices.

Section 3-4

25. **a.** *Research* Make a list of all the radio stations that broadcast in your area. Record each station's call letters, its number, whether it is AM or FM, and its category (such as country, top 40, classical, oldies, gospel, news/talk, and so on.)

    b. Use several types of data displays to look at different aspects of the information you collected in part (a). How can you use your displays to help you plan what to sell in your music store?

Section 3-5

27. *Group Activity* Work in a group of four students. Have each member of the group ask at least eight people how many

music recordings they bought in the last year. Keep track of the age of each person asked.

   a. Combine all the data and make a box-and-whisker plot.

   b. Divide the data into two groups: the answers from people under 20 years old and the answers from people 20 years old and over. Make a box-and-whisker plot for each group.

   c. Compare the plots you made in part (b). Which group usually buys more recordings? Which group has a greater range?

Section 3-6

24. a. *Research* Now you should have data on prices of recordings, types of radio stations, and the number of recordings people buy. What else do you want to know before completing a plan for a music store? Conduct a survey, collect data from magazines and newspapers, or contact local music organizations for information.

   b. *Open-ended* Choose a type of graph or display for each data set you have collected. Experiment with different types of displays.

Section 3-7

34. Use the data you have collected about the prices of recordings of different types of music on cassette, CD, and so on.

   a. Draw two graphs of the same data. Use one graph to show that cassettes, CDs, and so on have very different prices, and the other to show that cassettes, CDs, and so on have very similar prices.

   b. Which graph would you use to convince customers to buy one form of recording instead of another? Explain your choice.

Completing the Unit Project

Now you are ready to make your business brochure. You may want to use color or visual designs to make your brochure more attractive.

The plan you present in your brochure should include a summary of your market research. Include the percentage of your merchandise devoted to each music style and each format. To support your figures, describe the consumers in your store's area.

Include graphs and other data displays in your brochure. You may want to use a spreadsheet or other graphics software.

Look Back

Were the results of your research about popular styles and formats of music what you expected? Describe how your ideas about what is typical changed during the project.

Assessing the Unit Project

4 points The data collected are meaningful and support the plan for the business brochure. The graphs are appropriate for the presentation of the data and are drawn correctly. The brochure includes a summary of the market research and the percentages calculated are accurate. The visual design is attractive and original.

3 points The research is not complete and the resulting plan is somewhat incomplete. The graphs do not fully enhance the presentation of the results of the research. The visual design is acceptable but not particularly creative.

2 points The contents of the brochure are generally incomplete. The research is lacking substance and the data do not adequately support the plan. The graphs are not well drawn. The graphic design shows a lack of thought and effort.

1 point The brochure cannot be evaluated. The research is totally inadequate and the resulting plan does not support the decisions made. The group should be encouraged to speak with the teacher as soon as possible so that each student understands the purpose and the format of the project.

Alternative Projects

Project 1: Supporting an Opinion

One movie critic claims that the titles of popular movies in the 1970s were very short (*Jaws, Star Wars*) compared to titles of older movies (*Casablanca, Gone with the Wind*). Gather data and decide if you agree or disagree. Include these points in your report.

- how you decided what "popular" means in this case
- how you chose your data sets
- a summary of the data sets
- the process you used to make a decision
- the conclusion that your data supports

Project 2: Analyzing a Process

Find out how data are collected for making a Top Ten music, movie, or book list. Who supplies the data? Are any formulas used?

Write a summary of how the list is determined. Suggest how changes in the process could produce different results.

Outside Resources

McKean, Kevin. "The Fine Art of Reading Voters' Minds." *Discover*, May 1984.

"Data Analysis." *Mathematics Teacher*, February 1990.

Unit 4 Project
Making a Flip Book

Project Description

- The goal of this project is to have students discover how coordinates and the coordinate plane are used in real life through the creation of an animated flip book.
- Students will choose a picture to animate and then create the animation by slightly changing the coordinates of the critical points (vertices) of the picture. To begin, students should use graph paper of a convenient size and draw the first picture on the last sheet. A series of exercises throughout the unit will guide students as they work on their flip book.

Teaching Commentary

In this project, students use images to tell a story. Coordinates and functions are used to create a flip book. Mathematical skills and processes are applied to create the book which may or may not deal with a mathematical topic.

This project could be done by each student individually. If students are confident in the mathematics to be used and want to express their individuality, this project could provide a valuable experience. It could also be done by small groups or as a whole-class project.

Before the groups begin: Students should know how to locate points on a Cartesian coordinate system, and how to change an equation to move the graph of a function up, down, or sideways.

Cooperative work: Each group can produce a flip book, or the whole class can produce one book, with each group contributing a portion of the pages. In a class with widely different ability levels, small groups can take on a special, "expert" function. For example, one group could write the story, while others create the design, write equations, or check the finished product and suggest revisions.

Connections: An interesting extension of this activity is the exploration of geometric illusions and tessellations.

Working on the Unit Project Exercises

Section 4-1

A computer screen is made up of tiny points of light called *pixels*. Programmers use coordinates to identify which pixels to light when creating artwork. Different computers have different numbers of pixels.

---

36. **Writing** If you turn off the pixel at (4, 2) and turn on the one directly below it, it will look as if the pixel moved down.

   a. Describe how you could make the pixel "fall" to the bottom of the screen.

   b. How do the coordinates of the pixel change as it "falls"?

   c. Suppose you want to put a falling image in your flip book. Use your answers to parts (a) and (b) to describe how to do this.

Section 4-2

27. The diagrams below show a flip book sequence of parallelograms.

   a. Describe the motion the flip book shows. Which coordinates of the parallelograms change in the sequence? Which do not change?

   b. Find the areas of the parallelograms. Is one area larger than the others? If so, which one?

   c. *True or False?* All parallelograms with sides of the same length have the same area.

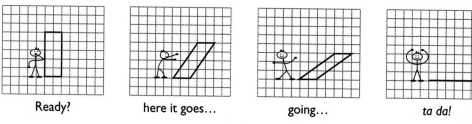

Ready?   here it goes...   going...   ta da!

Section 4-3

32. The pictures show a person dropping to the ground with a parachute. How do the coordinates of the parachute change as it approaches the ground?

33. **Open-ended** Draw a cartoon figure on a coordinate plane. Sketch two movements of the figure. Describe how the coordinates of the figure change as the figure moves.

34. Decide what your flip book will show. What types of motions will it use? Write a short description of your plan for the flip book.

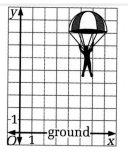
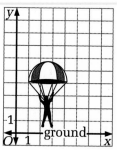

Section 4-4

25. Imagine making a flip book for each situation. Would you use a *translation* or a *rotation* to show each movement?

   a. a snail creeping along the ground

   b. an elevator arrow switching from "up" to "down"

26. **Open-ended** Describe a movement that could be shown by each transformation.

   a. translation

   b. rotation

Section 4-5

31. ***Research*** Read about how animation is created and used. As you read, you may want to take notes about animation ideas to help you as you make your flip book.

    Suggested Bibliography:

    Laybourne, Kit. *The Animation Book.* New York: Crown Publishers, 1979.

    Andersen, Yvonne. *Make Your Own Animated Movies.* Boston: Little, Brown and Company, 1970.

    Platt, Richard. *Film.* (Eyewitness Guides Series). London: Dorling Kindersley Limited, 1992, pp. 50–53.

Section 4-6

26. Start making the drawings for your flip book. Draw on graph paper to make sure the positions of your drawings are consistent. Keep track of the types of translations and rotations you use.

Section 4-7

45. Suppose you want your flip book to show a spaceship landing, then taking off again.

    a. ***Open-ended*** Which graph would you use to show the path of the spaceship?

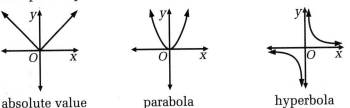

    absolute value   parabola   hyperbola

    b. Find the coordinates of five points on the graph that you chose.

    c. Make five separate diagrams of the spaceship, using the points that you found in part (b).

    d. Cut out the diagrams and make a 5-page flip book with them.

Completing the Unit Project

Now you are ready to finish your flip book.

- Complete your drawings. Put the pages in order and make sure that they are all the same size. Clip or staple the pages together.
- Write a script to narrate while the pages are being flipped.

Look Back

Describe how you used a coordinate system when making the drawings for your flip book. Did you have any problems making the flip book? If so, describe how you solved them.

Assessing the Unit Project

4 points Students have used their understanding of coordinates and functions successfully to create a flip book that shows a smooth continuous motion as the pages are flipped. Each picture is slightly different from the one before it. The drawings are accurate and the translations and rotations are used consistently to show the motion. The script is well-written and narrates the action accurately.

3 points Students understand the use of coordinates and functions to make the flip book. However, the motion is not always smooth and the positions of the drawings are not entirely consistent. The script is clear, but there is room for improvement.

2 points The flip book is essentially incomplete. The action is not continuous, and the use of the translations and rotations shows a lack of understanding of these concepts. The written narrative is at a minimal level. This project should be returned with suggestions for improvements and a new deadline given.

1 point This project cannot be evaluated. It is illegible or incomplete. The flip book should be returned with a new deadline for completion. The group should be encouraged to speak with the teacher as soon as possible so that each student understands the purpose and the format of the project.

Alternative Projects

Project 1: Making a Map

Create a map of the neighborhood around your school or of the neighborhood in which you live. Use a coordinate system and make a map key by listing the coordinates for the locations of the places on the map. Include a scale on your map.

Project 2: Recognizing Functions in Science

Read about the scientific research on global warming. Write a report on the latest findings. Discuss the evidence for global warming and what might be causing it. Include data tables and graphs with your report. Use the phrases "is a function of," "control variable," and "dependent variable" to describe the data.

Project 3: Collecting and Graphing Data

Collect data that can be displayed in a scatter plot. Write a report and include:

- the method(s) you used to gather the data
- a summary of the data
- a scatter plot of the data
- the type of correlation the scatter plot shows and the reasons for it
- several questions that can be answered using the scatter plot

Outside Resources

Disney Presents: Animation Studio. 1993 (IBM)

Animation Works. Goldstar Publications, 1992 (Macintosh)

Hypercard. Claris Publications

Linkway. (IBM)

Unit 5 Project
Planning a Car Wash

Project Description

- The goal of this project is to have students plan and organize a car wash as a fund-raising event. Students need to consider many variables in developing their plan of action.

  When planning a car wash, students decide which groups or organizations will receive the money raised, a location for the car wash, supplies needed, and the fee to be charged. They can begin by considering which groups or organizations they want to receive the funds raised and what location will attract the most customers. A series of exercises throughout the unit will guide students as they work on the car wash.

Teaching Commentary

This project calls for mathematical descriptions of a real-world problem. The problem of planning a car wash is translated into quantitative language and images in the hope that the process will result in a deeper understanding by students of both the problem and the mathematics involved. The project should be interesting to students because they will experience the solution first hand. It is open-ended (the actual profits cannot be known ahead of time), yet the validity of projections, predictions, and claims can be tested.

Before the groups begin: As homework, have students think about a worthwhile cause they would like to support in their community with the fund raiser. They may ask friends, parents, or neighbors for suggestions, or research areas of need by reading stories in local newspapers. A whole-class discussion should generate a list of considerations to be included in a plan. For example, students will want to generate a list of expenses that have to be taken into account in calculating the profit. The class should come to a consensus on the service to be provided with the money raised.

Cooperative work: Small-group work can be done in three stages. First, the groups can work on a plan of action for organizing and setting up the car wash. The plans of each group can be presented to the class. Second, the best ideas of all groups can be combined into one plan to be carried out by the entire class. The plan can include ways of dividing the work among the groups. Each group can have a different assignment to avoid duplication of effort. As the third stage, each group can create an exhibit of their contribution to the project.

Connections: A closely related topic, and one that many communities are involved in, is the United Way campaign. A history of the drives for the past five years, including goals, actual total contributions, and the amounts received by each organization can bring community needs and projects into sharper focus. Students can also analyze the budgets of public institutions, such as schools, hospitals, police, or fire departments.

You may wish to have students investigate the feasibility of starting a permanent car wash business, and create a mathematical model of the cash flow for the first five years of the business.

Working on the Unit Project Exercises

Section 5-1

36. a. In your group, set a reasonable goal of how much money your class wants to raise at the car wash.

  b. Make a table or spreadsheet to model your income if you charge $3 for each car you wash. Show the number of cars you need to wash to reach your goal.

  c. What is the effect on the number of cars you need to wash to reach your goal if you raise the price by $2? Lower the price by $2?

  d. What do you think is the highest price you can charge and still attract customers?

Section 5-2

37. a. In your group discuss ways you can advertise your car wash. Where are potential customers most likely to find out about the car wash?

  b. *Research* Find out the costs of your advertising options.

  c. Based on the costs and the number of potential customers you could reach, decide on two or three ways to advertise your car wash.

38. a. Make a list of supplies you will need for your car wash. Include advertising materials as well as cleaning supplies.

  b. *Research* Call or visit several stores to find the least expensive places to buy your supplies. Make a table to record the information.

Section 5-3

34. Write and solve an equation to find how many cars you have to wash to reach your goal if you charge:

  a. $3 per car

  b. $5 per car

  c. another price you are considering

35. a. Find the total cost for advertising and supplies based on your research.

  b. Write an equation to model your total income.

36. a. When your income equals your total expenses, you *break even*. Write and solve an equation to find out how many cars you need to wash at the price you are considering in order to break even.

  b. Is the number of cars you have to wash to break even a reasonable number? If you have to wash too many or too few cars, adjust your price and repeat part (a) until the number of cars you have to wash is reasonable.

Section 5-4

42. Write and solve an inequality to show how many cars you would have to wash at $5 per car to raise at least $300.

43. Write and solve an inequality to show how many cars you would have to wash at your price per car to at least reach your goal.

44. Write and solve an inequality to show how many cars you would have to wash at your price per car to raise more than you spend on supplies and advertising.

45. Decide on the price you will charge for each car you wash.

Section 5-5

32. Your *profit* from your car wash is your income minus your expenses. Your profit will depend on the number of customers you get.

    Write a formula for your profit after expenses.
    Let n = the number of cars you wash.

33. One way to estimate which location will have the most customers is to study traffic patterns. The number of cars on a certain street may depend on the day of the week or on the time of day.

    a. *Research* Design and carry out an experiment at your three location choices to estimate the number of customers you will have. Include different locations, days, and times.

    b. Summarize the results of your experiment. You may want to use a table or spreadsheet.

    c. Based only on the number of potential customers, which location is best? What are some reasons to choose another location?

    d. Choose one location to be the place for your car wash.

Section 5-6

30. Suppose one student can wash a car in 20 min. In one minute the student can wash $\frac{1}{20}$ of the car.

    rate of washing $= \frac{1}{20}$ car per minute

    a. What part of a car can 10 students working together wash in one minute?

    b. Do you think 20 students working together can wash a whole car in one minute? Why or why not?

31. a. *Research* Suppose a group of students is washing a car together.

    group's rate of washing $= \dfrac{1}{\text{group's time to wash a car}}$

    Experiment with different numbers of students. Find the different group rates of car washing. Decide how many people are needed to wash a car quickly and efficiently.

    b. Using a group the size you chose in part (a), how long will it take you to wash enough cars to reach your goal?

    c. Will there be enough time in one day for your group to reach your fund-raising goal if only one group of students washes cars? Why or why not?

    d. If you do not have enough time, what are some things you could do to reach your goal?

Section 5-7

28. Make a list of the number of students you need to work at the car wash. You may want to consider people for these jobs: advertisers, car washers, fee collectors, traffic controllers, and "runners" who bring dry towels and other supplies.

29. Make a diagram of the car wash area. Show where students will work. Also mark where you will have signs and the locations of supplies (including the location of the water supply). Make sure each student has a big enough work area.

30. Decide on the hours of your car wash. Make a schedule listing the jobs and the time periods. Write in the number of students needed for each job during each time period.

Section 5-8

28. **a.** The equation $P = I - E$ shows your profit after you subtract the expenses for the car wash from your income. Substitute your goal for P and your total expenses for E.

    b. Write an equation to represent your income after washing n cars at your price.

    c. Write a system of equations using your answers to parts (a) and (b).

    d. Solve the system you wrote in part (c) to find out how many cars you need to wash for your profit to equal your goal.

Completing the Unit Project

Now you are ready to present your plan of action. Your presentation should include reasons for your recommendations. Include these things in your presentation.

- a description of the best location for the car wash
- the price you have decided to charge for each car
- a list of the supplies you need and where you will purchase these items
- a discussion of how many cars you need to wash to break even
- a table showing your income and how many cars you need to wash to meet your fund-raising goal
- samples of advertisements and posters
- a diagram of the car wash area
- a list of the jobs and the number of people needed to run the car wash efficiently

Look Back

What did you learn from this project that can help you plan for future fund-raising events?

Assessing the Unit Project

4 points   The presentation is well organized and uses the mathematics developed in the unit appropriately. The plan of action includes the location and a diagram of the car wash, the charges for each car, supplies needed and where to purchase them, the number of cars necessary to break even and reach the fund-raising goal, sample advertisements, and the jobs and number of people needed to run the car wash. Reasons for these recommendations are included in the presentation.

3 points   The presentation is adequate but is not presented in a very well-organized manner. The details of the fundraising car wash are not as thorough as they should be.

2 points   The presentation is generally incomplete. The description of the location and the details of the necessary charges, supplies needed, or the number of cars needed to break even may be lacking. This project should be returned with suggestions for improvements and a new deadline.

1 point   This presentation cannot be evaluated. It is unorganized, illegible, or incomplete. The project should be returned with a new deadline for completion. The group should be encouraged to speak with the teacher as soon as possible so that students understand the purpose of the project.

Alternative Projects

Project 1: Working on Commission

Interview someone in a business to find out the salaries and commission rates for new salespeople and experienced salespeople.

Ask for some typical weekly or monthly sales figures. Make a table and a graph and write an equation for several different amounts of sales. Choose an income goal and figure out how many sales a new salesperson and an experienced salesperson need to earn that income.

Project 2: Researching Telephone Costs

Choose two locations you would like to call long distance. Decide on the time of day, the day of the week, and the length of each call. Contact two or three different long-distance telephone services to find out the cost for each call. Make a table and graph the data. Use the results to choose a long-distance service for your calls. Explain your choice.

Outside Resources

The local Chamber of Commerce, Small Business Administration, and Better Business Bureau have valuable information about the community's economic climate.

Numerous computer programs are available for creating spreadsheets and budgeting such as *Appleworks*, *Quicken*, *Lotus*, and *Excel*.

Unit 6 Project
Plan an Advertising Campaign

Project Description

- The goal of this project is to have students plan an advertising campaign for a product or service that is appealing to students in their school.

- When planning the advertisements, students choose what to advertise, decide which media to use, compare the unit costs for different media, and then either write a script or draw a sketch of the ad. They can begin by discussing the kinds of products and services students in their school may like. A series of exercises throughout the unit will guide students as they work on the campaign.

Teaching Commentary

This project involves students in a significant aspect of their environment, namely, advertising. It requires that they understand and use mathematical concepts to predict the preferences of consumers. In so doing, students interpret statistical data and design a way of reaching and convincing potential consumers. Statistical reasoning, inductive reasoning, and analogy are used throughout.

Before the groups begin: Group members should begin by having a preliminary discussion of ideas that can provide a basis for their research. They need to ask themselves questions such as: What would I like to see in the cafeteria that is not available at this time? Are others likely to have the same wish? Their research should take the form of observations. Each student should also make a list of advertisements seen during a predetermined period of time and collect and bring to school examples of magazine and newspaper ads.

Cooperative work: Each group should first decide on a product or service and then design a questionnaire for market research. Students can then gather data and keep the product or service or choose a different one based on their data. Once a product/service is selected, students can design an advertising campaign for it. They can then examine the size or length of the ad, the images used, and to whom the ad is directed.

Connections: Advertising is a rich source of information about economic and societal trends and values. It may be correlated to historical events and reflect predominant artistic styles. The use of mathematics in advertising (geometric shapes, numerical expressions, statistical claims) is also an interesting topic to explore in connection with this project. Ads can be very useful for developing critical thinking skills by providing many examples of the ways in which they may or may not be misleading.

Working on the Unit Project Exercises

Section 6-1

17. **Research** Keep a daily record of the TV programs you watch and the magazines and newspapers you read.

   a. List the name of each TV program you watch, the day and time you watch it, and the products advertised during commercial breaks.

   b. List each magazine or newspaper you look at or read, and the products in the ads you look at or read.

Section 6-2

Use the table.

34. a. Suppose a movie is showing on television. Find the probability that a movie viewer picked at random is an adult woman and the probability that the viewer is an adult man.

   b. Which event from part (a) has the greater probability? Are these complementary events? Why or why not?

35. Based on the data in the table, what kind of show do you think is most popular with teenagers? Give a reason for your answer.

36. Give two examples of how an advertiser could use the data shown.

Viewers (Thousands)

	Drama	Suspense/ Mystery	Comedy	News 6–7 P.M.	Movies
Women	9020	10,370	10,560	7270	10,730
Men	5890	7320	6530	5470	7230
Teens (12–17)	820	740	2070	380	1130
Children (2–11)	1400	1450	3400	790	1570
Total	17,130	19,880	22,560	13,910	20,660

Section 6-3

38. a. A typical cost for a 30-second commercial during prime time on network television is $100,000. At this rate, what would you expect the cost of a 45-second commercial to be?

   b. Suppose a 30-second commercial will reach 300,000 teenage viewers. What is the cost per viewer?

39. **Research** Find the cost of a full-page ad in a local newspaper and how many copies of the newspaper are sold in a day. What is the cost per reader?

40. a. What do you think are some advantages of advertising on television? in a newspaper?

   b. Why is it important for the advertiser to know the reading and viewing habits of the people who will buy the product?

Section 6-4

17. **Group Activity** Work with the whole class.

   a. Use the daily records of television and newspaper or magazine ads kept by you and your classmates. Which TV programs, magazines, and newspapers are the most popular? What types of25

   products are advertised on or in them?

  b. ***Research*** Find out the total number of students in your school. Using your class as a sample, estimate the total number of students who watch the most popular programs and read the most popular magazines and newspapers.

  c. Do you think the daily records kept by you and your classmates is a good sample for predicting the viewing and reading habits of teenagers throughout the country? Why or why not?

Section 6-5

The cost of a newspaper ad is usually related to its size. The size is measured in *column inches*. One column inch is $2\frac{1}{16}$ in. wide (the width of one column of print in the newspaper) and 1 in. long.

 32. a. An ad spreads across 2 columns and is 4 in. deep. Another ad spreads across 4 columns and is 2 in. deep. Are the ads similar? Explain.

   b. Which of the ads described in part(a) has a greater area?

 33. In one newspaper, a full-page ad is 216 column inches. Is it similar to a quarter-page ad? to a half-page ad? Explain why or why not.

Section 6-6

 24. a. Make a sketch of an ad for your product or trace a simple ad. Dilate the sketch with a scale factor of 2 and a center of dilation at one corner of the ad. Which size is more effective, the original or the enlargement?

   b. Suppose you want to put the ad on a billboard. What scale factor might you use?

Section 6-7

 29. ***Research*** Find the costs of advertising in at least three of these media.

- your local newspaper
- your school newspaper
- the magazines you read
- a local radio station
- a local TV station
- some other source

Completing the Unit Project

Now you are ready to use the data you collected to plan your advertising campaign. Your plan should include the following information.

- a description of the product or service you are advertising and the data that supports your choice of product
- your decision about where to advertise your product or service and the data that supports your choice of media
- a schedule of when and how often your ad will run

Project Book, INTEGRATED MATHEMATICS 1

- an estimate of the cost of running your ad on the media you selected
- either a sketch of a print ad or a script for a TV or radio ad

Look Back

Did your classmates all make the same decisions or were there many different results? Discuss why people may develop different plans even though they all target the same market segment.

Assessing the Unit Project

4 points   The advertising campaign is well organized. The written plan describes the product or service thoroughly and has supporting data. The unit costs and use of probability concepts are applied correctly. The choice of advertising media, its schedule, and the estimated cost is appropriate. The media ad sketch or script is appealing.

3 points   The advertising campaign is acceptable but is not fully supported by the data. Some key features of the plan are missing. The written plan is not as thorough as possible. The media ad may be appealing, but some improvements are possible.

2 points   The advertising campaign is incomplete. The written plan is incomplete and not supported by the data. The media ad is incomplete or unclear. This project should be returned with suggestions for improvements and a new deadline.

1 point   The advertising campaign cannot be evaluated. It is illegible or incomplete. The plan should be returned with a new deadline for completion. The group should be encouraged to speak with the teacher so that they understand the purpose and the format of the project.

Alternative Projects

Project 1: Changing the Rules

Use a game in which dice are thrown to determine the players' moves around a game board. Find the probabilities of several events in the game.

Change the rules of the game. How does this affect the probabilities? Present your conclusions in an oral report. Display the results on a poster.

Project 2: Finding Ratios

In a golden rectangle, the ratio $\frac{\text{length}}{\text{width}}$ is about 1.618. This is called the *golden ratio*.

- Research the history of the golden ratio. Find its exact value.
- Find examples of the golden ratio in art and architecture.
- Measure rooms, pictures, and furniture. Do any use the golden ratio?
- Summarize your results. Make a visual display

Outside Resources

Grillo, Paul Jacques. *Form, Function and Design.* New York: Dover Publications, 1960.

Fleming, William. *Arts and Ideas.* New York: Holt, Rinehardt and Winston, 1980.

Data Analysis. Department of Mathematics and Computer Science, North Carolina School of Science and Mathematics, 1988. Available through the NCTM, Reston, VA. (materials and software)

Unit 7 Project
Design a Sports Arena

Project Description

- The goal of this project is to have students make a two-dimensional scale drawing or a three-dimensional model of a sports arena for skateboard or in-line skating competitions.

  When designing an arena, students decide on the number and slope of the ramps, the arc lengths of any circular parts, the materials needed, and the estimated cost of building the arena. Students can begin by considering the overall design of the arena. A series of exercises throughout the unit will guide students as they work on the arena.

Teaching Commentary

This project involves an application of mathematics to a real-world problem. Students apply the mathematics they learn in the unit to the design of the arena. Students need to understand the design features of the arena, and also they need to know how to create a two- or three-dimensional model of it. They will be using inductive reasoning through the process of trial and error.

Before the groups begin: Have students write a short description of any skating or skateboarding experience they have had, or of any skating or skateboarding event they have seen in person, on television, or in a film. Based on this description, students can generate ideas about the factors they need to take into consideration when building a rink. Then, when students get together with their group members, they will each have some images and ideas to contribute.

Cooperative work: Drawing a scale model is an excellent activity, though not always an easy one. An alternative to the two-dimensional representation of the rink would be a three-dimensional scale model, including "scale" people. The advantage of such a model is that students can test their designs and see why certain sizes work or not. In addition to costing out the actual arena, students should cost out the model. This will give them some practical experience with financial planning on a small scale.

Connections: This project could be done as an interdisciplinary unit with physics, business, social studies, or writing. For example, students could keep a journal of all work, including the sequence of activities, problems encountered, solutions tried, successes, failures, and explanations for each. The journal should include mathematical explanations and diagrams. This gives students practice in communicating about the world using mathematical ideas.

Working on the Unit Project Exercises

Section 7-1

27. Suppose you decide to construct a straight skateboard ramp that makes an angle of 8° with the ground.

   a. How long would the base of the ramp have to be in order to reach a height of 3 ft above the ground?

   b. If you do not have enough space for a ramp that long, should you increase or decrease the angle? What is the disadvantage for the skater if you design the ramp this way?

   c. Explain why a curved ramp might be better than a straight ramp.

Section 7-2

32. **Research** Why is urethane used in making wheels for skateboards and inline skates? How are the properties of urethane related to a bouncing ball?

Section 7-3

29. A "half-pipe" skateboard ramp is formed by two quarter-circle ramps with a flat space in between. The ramps reach a height of 11 ft and are 16 ft apart. Find the distance a skateboarder travels from the top of one ramp to the top of the other ramp.

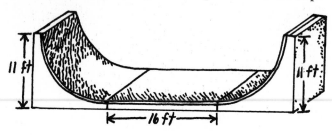

Section 7-4

43. The frictional force on an in-line skater's wheels varies directly with the skater's weight.

   a. A 150 lb skater experiences 40.5 lb of friction when skating on a dry steel surface. Find the variation constant.

   b. Write a direct variation equation for this situation.

   c. Find the frictional force on a 130 lb skater.

   d. The variation constant for skating on a wet steel surface is 0.23. Is this greater or less than the variation constant you found in part (a)? Does this make sense?

   e. What kind of surfaces should you consider in your plans for a skateboard ramp?

Section 7-5

36. One plan for building a skateboard launch ramp calls for 4 sheets of $\frac{5}{8}$ in. plywood, one sheet of $\frac{3}{8}$ in. plywood, and one sheet of $\frac{1}{8}$ in. plywood. All the sheets measure 4 ft by 8 ft. Find the total cost of purchasing the plywood needed for this ramp.

Thickness of plywood	Cost per square foot
$\frac{5}{8}$ in.	$.66
$\frac{3}{8}$ in.	$.47
$\frac{1}{8}$ in.	$.34

37. **Research** List the materials you would need to build the ramps for your skating arena. Check with a local lumber yard to find current prices. Estimate the cost of the materials you would need.

Section 7-6

34. To make the sides of a skateboard ramp, two corner-to-corner arcs are drawn from opposite corners of a plywood square. The wood where the sectors overlap is not used.

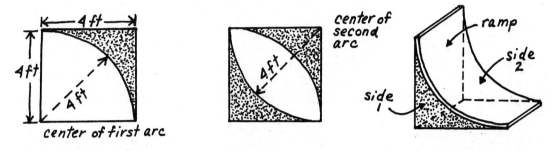

    a. What is the area of each side of the ramp?

    b. What is the area of the plywood not used?

    c. What fraction of the plywood square is not used?

35. A circular arena for skaters includes a skating rink with a radius of 30 ft. There are benches in a circle 10 ft beyond the edge of the rink.

    a. Find the total area of the arena, including the space between the rink and the benches.

    b. Find the area of the space between the rink and the benches.

Completing the Unit Project

Now you are ready to complete a scale drawing or a model of your skating competition arena. Label its parts and the dimensions.

Include answers to these questions on your drawing or in a description of your model.

- What are the slopes of the ramps used in your arena?
- What are the arc lengths of any of the circular parts of your arena?
- What is the slope of the bleachers?
- What materials are needed to build your arena?
- What is the estimated cost of building your arena?

Look Back

Write an evaluation of each arena designed by your class. What features do many of the designs have in common? What features are unique? Which designs do you like the best? Why?

Assessing the Unit Project

4 points The scale drawing or model is drawn or made correctly. The parts and dimensions are labeled correctly. The slopes of the ramps are realistic, as is the slope of the bleachers. The overall design of the arena is functional and the cost estimates are appropriate.

3 points The scale drawing or model meets the criteria for the project, but certain details are lacking or are somewhat incomplete. There are minor mathematical errors involving the slopes of the ramps or in the calculations of the arc lengths. The cost estimates may be slightly too high or too low.

2 points The scale drawing or model of the arena and its description contain serious errors or are incomplete. Not all of the questions asked are answered, and there is little understanding of the mathematics involved in the project.

1 point This project cannot be evaluated. It is illegible, incomplete, or not understandable. The scale drawing or model should be returned with a new deadline for completion. The group should be encouraged to speak with the teacher as soon as possible so that they understand the purpose and format of the project.

Alternative Projects

Project 1: A Trip to Another Country

Write a story about a trip to another country. Include how you might use direct variation during the trip. For example, show how the cost of a car rental varies with mileage, how to convert distances between cities from kilometers to miles, and how to change dollars into the currency of another country.

Project 2: The History of π

Research the number π. What are some of the approximations for π that have been used by different cultures? How many digits of π are known?

Outside Resources

The Challenge of the Unknown: "Speed Skiing: Going for the Limit." Phillips Petroleum, 1986. Available from Karol Media, 3101 Geospace Drive, Independence, MO 64056-1700. (free video and accompanying book)

Sportsworks. Toronto: Ontario Science Center, 1989.

MacMotion. Vernier Software.

Interactive Physics. Knowledge Revolution. (Macintosh)

Unit 8 Project
Predicting the Future

Project Description

- **The goal of this project is to have students write a news article and predict the new record-breaking time for a swimming event.**

  When writing the article, students use mathematical models to analyze past Olympic results to help predict the new record. To begin, students can think about how they will organize the data they collect and whether they will be able to use a computer database or spreadsheet. A series of exercises throughout the unit will guide students as they work on the article.

Teaching Commentary

This project gives students an excellent opportunity to understand the nature of probability, statistics, and the uncertainties associated with making future predictions based upon historical data. They need to understand that very often it is not possible to have all the information or understand all the variables that may affect the prediction of future events. Predictions can be made with greater or lesser certainty depending on how complete our knowledge is of the variables influencing the outcome.

Before the groups begin: Have students brainstorm about their own experiences in some sport or in the acquisition of some skill. Ask if they could have predicted their level of proficiency or ability before they started working on improving. Have student athletes share with the class the story of their skill development in specific sports.

Cooperative work: It may be useful to pair students according to their interests. Writers can share their experiences in self-expression. Athletes as a group would have shared experiences, as would artists, musicians, or actors. Be sure to have students share their ideas in class. The recognition of a similar experience can create a sense of community and increase respect among students. Students should also draw graphs of their personal experiences and create mathematical functions that represent the graphs.

Connections: An interesting extension to this project's activities would be speculation about where each student will be in five or ten years. Students can also predict how tall siblings or other small children they know will be at age 18. They should justify their predictions based on statistical data, draw graphs of the growth, and list sources of errors.

Working on the Unit Project Exercises

Section 8-1

44. Use the data on page 416 for the Olympic 400 m freestyle swimming race.

    a. Find the slope of the line between 1972 and 1976 for the women.

    b. Find the slope of the line between 1972 and 1976 for the men.

    c. *Writing* Did the men or the women show more improvement in their times between 1972 and 1976? Describe two different ways you can justify your choice.

    d. *Writing True or False?* The rates of change in men's and women's times have been negative for the Olympic data. Describe how this is shown in the graph of data. How is it shown in the table?

Section 8-2

27. *Research* Find another set of winning times for the 400 m freestyle for the years shown in the table on page 416. You might look for world records, college records, or high school records. Find both men's and women's records.

Section 8-3

36. The winning times in the 400 m swimming event at the Olympics has changed over the years. What numerical aspect of the event has *not* changed over time? Draw a graph that shows this.

Section 8-4

31. *Group Activity* Use the winning times for the women's 400 m freestyle swimming race in the Olympics on page 416. Use *years after 1960* as the control variable. Have each person write an equation to model the data. Compare equations. Does one equation fit the data better than the other? Decide which equation you will use to model the data.

Section 8-5

30. The equations of the fitted lines for the graphs of some California high school record times are given. In the equations, x is the number of years since 1957 and y is the record time in seconds.

    a. Use a graph to estimate a solution of the system of equations.

    b. Use substitution to find a solution.

    c. What do the coordinates of the solution mean?

> **Girls' 400 m Individual Medley:**
> $y = -1.95x + 335.05$
> **Boys' 400 m Individual Medley:**
> $y = -1.68x + 299.1$

Section 8-6

39. Look at the graph of the winning times for men's 400 m freestyle swimming on page 439. Which points clearly lie below the fitted line? Which years do they represent? Write an inequality to describe the region below the fitted line.

Section 8-7

39. *Group Activity* Use the data you researched in Section 8-2.

    a. Compare the data you found to the Olympic data on page 416. Which values are greater? Which are less? Which are equal?

    b. Have one person graph the men's winning times and the other graph the women's. Put *Years after 1960* on the horizontal axis.

    c. For each graph, decide whether there is a negative correlation between the winning times and the number of years since 1960. If so, draw a fitted line and write an equation to model the data.

Completing the Unit Project

Now you can analyze the trends in the Olympic swimming data. Make each of these predictions.

- In what year will the men's and women's winning times for the 400 m freestyle event be equal?
- How will the men's and women's times compare in the years after their times are equal?
- In what year will the women's 400 m freestyle record be broken? What do you think the new record will be?

Write your news article predicting the new record-breaking time for the women's 400 m freestyle swimming event. Use graphs to present some of the information in your article.

Look Back

How accurate do you think your predictions are? List some reasons why the model you used may not be suitable for making long-term predictions. Keep your news article and data file. Watch the news to see whether your predictions come true!

Assessing the Unit Project

4 points   The news article predicting a new Olympic swimming record is clearly written and supported by data displays. The trends of past Olympic swimming events are analyzed and incorporated in the article. The mathematical models chosen are used correctly to make a prediction. The writing style is creative and appropriate for the readers of the newspaper or magazine.

3 points   The news article is adequate. The data displays have not been analyzed as thoroughly as they could have been. The data file has minor problems in supporting the information included in the article.

2 points   The news article is incomplete. It is not supported in large part by the data displays or analysis of past Olympic events. This project should be returned with suggestions for improvements and a new deadline.

1 point The news article cannot be evaluated. It is illegible, incomplete, or not understandable. The project should be returned with a new deadline for completion. Students should be encouraged to speak with the teacher as soon as possible so that they understand the purpose and the format of the project.

Alternative Projects

Project 1: Playing the Market

Use a stock market report from a newspaper and "invest" $1000 in a stock of your choice. Check the paper every day and record the value of your stock. At the end of a week, graph the data and find an equation for a fitted line.

Find out what the interest rate is for a savings account at a bank and calculate how much interest $1000 will earn in one week.

Write a report to present your findings. Include answers to these questions: Do you think investing money in stock is better than leaving it in a bank? Why or why not? Is this a good way to decide how to invest?

Project 2: Projected Savings

Research a long-term payment plan for a car or another item. Find out the initial payment, the monthly payments, and the number of months in the plan.

Model the plan with a graph and an equation. Write a report that describes your model. Include answers to these questions: Suppose you saved the amount of money needed to pay the total cost all at once. When could you buy the item? How much money would you save by not paying interest with monthly payments? Which payment plan is the best? Why?

Outside Resources

Tanur, Judith M., ed. *Statistics: A Guide to the Unknown*. Pacific Grove, CA: Wadsworth and Brooks/Cole, Advanced Books and Software, 1989.

The Physics Explorer. Wings for Learning. (Macintosh)

Unit 9 Project
Build Your Own Boat

Project Description

- The goal of this project is to have students build a cardboard boat using a milk or juice carton.
- After making the boat, students use mathematical skills they have learned in this unit to predict the draft and the amount of cargo the boat will hold. Then they check their predictions by floating the boat. To begin, students can collect an empty milk or juice carton to build their boat. A series of exercises throughout the unit will guide students as they work on their boats.

Teaching Commentary

This project is excellent for exploring mathematics in an interdisciplinary context. It involves a physical activity that at first can be explored informally. Then the work can be refined and reproduced when the successes and failures are explained mathematically. In using experiments and models to create an understanding of mathematical generalizations, induction and analogy are the primary types of reasoning employed.

Before the groups begin: Students can do independent research on boat shapes and designs. They may find materials in the library, in the media, or if they live near water, in their environment. Toy or hobby shops may also give them valuable ideas.

Cooperative work: Have students share their ideas with their partners. They should keep a journal of their experiments and insights. They should also generate a list of observations and factors influencing the outcomes, explain each mathematically, and try to formulate generalizations about density, buoyancy, and material strength.

Connections: Historical connections are natural ones for this project. The development of different types of boats and ships in different cultures throughout history is fascinating and provides a good thread for understanding connections between science and society. There is also a wealth of literature, poetry, and music associated with boats, which can provide a good link between science and the humanities.

Working on the Unit Project Exercises

Section 9-1

36. *Group Activity* Work with another student. You will need a ruler, scissors, and a protractor. You will use your results in Exercise 37 on page 491.

   a. Draw any isosceles triangle.

   b. *Using Manipulatives* Cut out the isosceles triangle. Fold the triangle to line up the sides of equal length.

   c. Open up your triangle. Measure all the angles and segments. You may want to record the measurements in a table.

   d. Draw at least three other isosceles triangles. Repeat parts (a)–(c) for each new triangle.

   e. *Writing* Describe what you have learned about isosceles triangles from parts (a)–(d). Did you use inductive or deductive reasoning?

   f. Write a formula for finding *h* if you know *a* and *b*. Write any fraction in the formula in decimal form for easy use on a calculator.

Section 9-2

Use the empty milk carton or other container you collected.

  36. Construct a boat using these steps.

   a. Open the top of the carton completely.

   b. Cut through two opposite side edges and along a diagonal of the base of the carton.

   c. Use either half of the carton to construct a boat with triangular ends.

  37. **a.** Measure the sides and height of a triangular end of the boat you built.

   b. Explain why you can use the formula you found in Exercise 36 on page 485 to approximate the height of a triangular end of your boat.

   c. Test the formula you wrote in Exercise 36 on page 485. How close is the height from the formula to the measured height you found in part (a)?

Section 9-3

For Exercises 47–49, tell whether you think each statement is *True* or *False*. Give a reason for your choice.

  47. If a boat has a hole in it, the boat sinks.

  48. If an object can float in fresh water, the object can float in salt water.

  49. If an object is made of steel, the object cannot float in water.

  50. Write the converse of each statement in Exercises 47–49. Tell whether you think the converse is *True* or *False*. Give a reason for your choice.

  51. Gather some small objects (for example, a coin, a pencil, a toothpick, a paper clip, a piece of paper, cardboard, wood, or string). Tell whether you think the probability is 0 or 1 that each object will float in a pan of water. Then test your predictions.

Section 9-4

  19. *Research* Read the entry on *water* in an encyclopedia or a science book.

   a. What is the weight in grams of 1 cubic centimeter of water?

   b. What is the weight in pounds of one cubic foot of water?

   c. What does H_2O stand for?

   d. Is ice heavier than water?

20. *Research* Read the entry on *buoyancy* in an encyclopedia or a science book. Describe what determines the buoyancy of an object.

Section 9-5

31. What type of space figure is your boat?

32. **a.** Make a sketch of your boat. Record its measurements in centimeters. (Use the conversion factor 1 in. = 2.54 cm if necessary.)

    b. Find the area of a triangular base of your boat.

Section 9-6

Imagine your boat floating in the water. Part of the boat will be below the water level. Here are two scientific facts that you may have learned in your research on buoyancy and water.

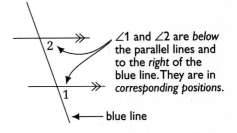

B = area of part of base that is under water

> When an object floats in the water, the object sinks until the weight of the water it displaces equals the weight of the object.
>
> Since 1 cm³ of water weighs 1 g, the volume of any amount of water (in cubic centimeters) equals the weight of the water (in grams).

29. The weight of your milk carton boat is about 35 g. Later, you will add 300 cm³ of water to your boat to make it stable.

    a. What is the weight of 300 cm³ of water?

    b. What will be the total weight of your boat with the added water?

    c. What will be the weight of the water your boat will displace when it floats?

    d. What volume of water will your boat displace?

    e. When you float your boat, the part under water will be shaped like a triangular prism as shown above. Complete this equation: $Bh = $ __?__ .

    f. Find B for your boat

Section 9-7

23. **a.** Draw two parallel lines and a third line that crosses them. Label the angles as shown.
        Measure ∠1 and ∠2. What do you notice?

    b. Draw another pair of parallel lines with a third line that crosses them. Draw the third line at a different angle than you used above. Find and measure two angles that are in corresponding positions the way ∠1 and ∠2 are in this diagram. What do you notice?

    c. Repeat part (b) several times.

    d. Make a conjecture about the measures of angles in corresponding positions when a line crosses two parallel lines.

∠1 and ∠2 are *below* the parallel lines and to the *right* of the blue line. They are in *corresponding positions.*

blue line

24. The diagram below shows one triangular base of your boat. When your boat is in the water, a portion of the base ($\triangle XYT$) will be under water. As long as the boat is level, $\overline{XY}$ will be parallel to $\overline{RS}$.

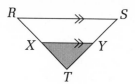

   a. How is $\overline{RT}$ like the blue line in the diagram in Exercise 23?

   b. Using the conjecture that you made in part (d) of Exercise 23, what can you say about $\angle TXY$ and $\angle R$?

   c. What can you say about $\angle XTY$ and $\angle RTS$? Why?

   d. What two triangles in the diagram are similar? How do you know?

25. Use a ruler to mark a centimeter scale along the height of one triangular base of your boat. Include a scale mark at least every 5 mm. Describe how you can use the scale to find the *draft* of your boat (see page 474) when it is in the water.

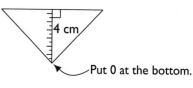

Put 0 at the bottom.

Section 9-8

32. Label a sketch of one base of your boat as shown. $\triangle XYT$ is the part of the base that will be under water when you float your boat.

Use your results of earlier *Working on the Unit Project* exercises to complete each statement.

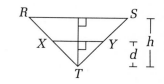

   a. From part (b) of Exercise 32 on page 514, area of $\triangle RST = \underline{\quad?\quad}$.

   b. From part (f) of Exercise 29 on page 522, area of $\triangle XYT = \underline{\quad?\quad}$.

   c. From part (a) of Exercise 37 on page 491, height of $\triangle RST$, $h = \underline{\quad?\quad}$.

33. In Exercise 24 on page 529 you discovered that $\triangle RST \sim \triangle XYT$.

   a. Use the values from Exercise 32 to write a proportion to find d, the height of $\triangle XYT$.

   b. Solve your proportion for d.

   c. Explain why your answer to part (b) is the *draft* of your boat.

Completing the Unit Project

Now you are ready to find the actual draft of the boat you built.

- Fill your boat with 300 cm³ of water and float the boat in a large sink or container.

- Read the boat's draft from the scale that you marked on your boat. Record your results.

Now you can determine how much cargo your boat can carry.

- Select one object for the first test and predict how many of these objects will cause your boat to sink.

- Record your predictions and then test your guesses by filling your boat with these objects.

- Count how many items your boat can hold until it sinks and record these results.

When you have gathered data from at least three cargo tests, describe your observations in a report. Include the effect of the size of the object, the relative heaviness of the object, and the number of each object it took to sink your boat.

Look Back

Get together with a small group of students. Share your results. Discuss these questions: How close is the actual draft to your prediction? Why might the actual draft and the predicted draft be different? What have you learned about buoyancy?

Assessing the Unit Project

4 points The boat is well made. Student predictions of the boat's actual draft and how much cargo it can carry are supported by appropriate data. All calculations are error free. A thorough description of the observations of the cargo tests is included in the folder. The project notes are thorough and complete.

3 points The boat is adequately made. The predictions of the draft and cargo capacity are not thoroughly supported by the data. Some of the calculations contain minor errors. The written report does not describe the cargo test observations as completely as it should.

2 points The boat is incomplete. The predictions of the draft and cargo capacity are incomplete or inaccurate. The report of the cargo tests may need more elaboration. This project should be returned with suggestions for improvements and a new deadline.

1 point This project cannot be evaluated. It is illegible, incomplete, or not understandable. The report should be returned with a new deadline for completion. Students should be encouraged to speak with the teacher as soon as possible so that they understand the purpose and the format of the project.

Alternative Projects

Project 1: Boating in Various Seas

Water takes up less space as it starts to cool but more space as it freezes. Write a story on how this affects the draft of a boat passing through the Arctic, through the North Atlantic, through the Panama Canal, and across the Equator.

Project 2: Design a Container

Create a design for a container to keep things hot or cold. First, decide what objects you want to carry in your container and then plan a shape to fit those objects. Keep in mind that a container with a large surface area relative to its volume will generally lose heat faster than one with a smaller surface area.

Outside Resources

Lloyd, G. E. R. *Early Greek Science: Thales to Aristotle*. Chatto & Windus, 1970.

Neugebauer, O. *The Exact Sciences in Antiquity*. New York: Dover Publications, 1969.

Epstein, Lewis Carroll. *Thinking Physics: Practical Lessons in Critical Thinking*. San Francisco: Insight Press, 1991.

Adney, Edwin Tappan and Howard Chapelli. *The Bark Conoes and Skin Boats of North America*. Washington, D.C., Smithsonian Institution, 1983.

The Challenge of the Unknown: "Canoe Building: A Balancing Act." Phillips Petroleum, 1986. Available from Karol Media, 3101 Geospace Drive, Independence, MO 64056-1700. (free video and accompanying book)

Unit 10 Project
Write a Math Story

Project Description

- The goal of this project is to have students write a math story that includes at least three situations that are modeled by equations or formulas from earlier units and one situation that is modeled by an equation from this unit.
- When writing the story, students choose the setting, characters, and plot, along with the equations and formulas studied in the course that can be used in the story. Students can begin by thinking of a setting for their story and start work on an outline. A series of exercises throughout the unit will guide students as they work on their stories.

Teaching Commentary

This project brings together several aspects of the previous project. It calls for mathematical descriptions and representations of real-world situations, and it builds on the mathematics learned in the course. The model it requires is not static, but incorporates process and change. It is also interdisciplinary and requires creativity. It may be a good idea to start an ongoing anthology of the stories written by the groups. If this becomes a regular activity, each year the groups can get inspiration from the stories already written, and add their new stories to the collection.

Before the groups begin: Have students write a brief outline or description of their favorite sports story or experience. In so doing, they will have ideas when they start working in groups.

Cooperative work: Perhaps the best method of collaboration for this project is some version of the *jigsaw*. The project has several aspects, requiring different talents or specializations. Each group can have a writer, an illustrator, a grapher, and an editor/checker. Specialists from each group can get together (forming an expert group) to discuss ideas, problems, and solutions relating to their group's stories, then return to their home groups with new ideas for revisions.

An alternative format for this project would have the whole class engage in writing one story. In this case, you would have groups of specialists working on the same story. You could have a team of writers, as well as an editing team, checking on the written and mathematical content. A computational team would be responsible for the equations, graphs, and other mathematical operations. The illustrators would bring the story alive through pictures. You could even have a team of actors, acting out the story to the class or to the whole school.

Connections: A link to history, literature, arts, sciences, and mathematics is very easily established here. The project would be an excellent one for developing an interdisciplinary or multidisciplinary unit.

Working on the Unit Project Exercises

Section 10-1

31. *Group Activity* Work in a group of three students. Two of you should toss a ball back and forth in front of a wall while the third observes the path of the ball (you can use a crumpled piece of paper for a ball). Toss the ball a few different ways, and take turns until each student has had a chance to be the observer.

    a. Each of you should make a sketch of one path that he or she observed.

    b. Does the path you drew have symmetry? If so, sketch the line of symmetry.

    c. Compare everyone's drawings. How are they alike? How are they different?

Section 10-2

53. Suppose the origin on a coordinate plane represents the point where a baseball is hit. Which equation has a graph that might be the path of the baseball? Explain how you made your choice.

    A. $y = x^2$

    B. $y = (x - 10)^2 + 100$

    C. $y = -x^2$

    D. $y = -(x - 10)^2 + 100$

54. For the graph you chose in Exercise 53, write the equation of the line of symmetry and the coordinates of the vertex.

Section 10-3

25. Suppose a batter hits a ball that is very low to the ground. The ball lands at a spot 100 ft away.

    a. Suppose the ball is hit from the ground. Sketch a graph of a possible path of the ball. Use the x-axis as the ground and the origin as the point where the ball was hit.

    b. What are the x-intercepts of your path?

    c. Is there more than one possible path with these intercepts? Explain.

    d. Could the graph of the equation $y = -x(x - 100)$ represent the ball's path? Describe your reasoning.

Section 10-4

43. *Research* The pull of gravity is not the same on every planet. Do some research on how this affects a ball thrown or dropped on other planets.

Section 10-5

41. One equation for the path of a ball hit at a 45° angle is $y = x(1 - 0.005x)$.

    a. Find the x-intercepts of the graph of the equation.

    b. What do the x-intercepts represent in this equation?

    c. Write the expanded form of the equation.

Project Book, INTEGRATED MATHEMATICS 1

42. Another equation for the path of a ball hit at a 45° angle is
$y = -0.003x^2 + x$.

    a. Write the factored form of the equation.

    b. Find the x-intercepts of the graph of the equation.

    c. In this situation, what is represented by the x-intercepts?

43. Which of the equations in Exercises 41 and 42 represents the
path of the ball that lands farther away? What do you think made
it land farther away?

Section 10-6

41. An equation for the path of a ball hit at a 45° angle with an initial
speed of 80 ft/s is $y = -0.005x^2 + x$. Find each feature of the
graph of this equation.

    a. the y-intercept

    b. the equation of the line of symmetry

    c. the coordinates of the vertex

    d. the maximum height reached by the ball

42. Suppose you repeated Exercise 41 with the equation
$y = -0.005x^2 + x + 4$. Predict how the results would be
different. Then repeat Exercise 41 with this equation and check
your prediction.

Section 10-7

43. **Baseball** An equation for the path of a baseball hit at a 45° angle
with an initial speed of about 103 ft/s is $y = -0.003x^2 + x + 4$.
In factored form, this equation can be approximated by
$y = -0.003(x + 4)(x - 337)$.

    a. At what height off the ground is the ball hit ? Which form of
    the equation helps you answer this question most easily?

    b. How far from home plate will the ball hit the ground? Which
    form of the equation helps you answer this question most
    easily?

    c. Suppose the left field fence is 325 ft from home plate and
    stands ten feet high. Will a ball hit down the left field line go
    over the fence? Why or why not?

Section 10-8

34. An equation for the path of a baseball hit at a 50° angle with an
initial speed of 80 ft/s is $y = -0.006x^2 + 1.192x + 4$. How far
from home plate will the ball hit the ground?

35. When a baseball is hit at a 45° angle, the equation $r = \dfrac{v^2}{32}$ gives
the *range*, how far away the ball hits the ground. In the equation,
v represents the initial speed of the ball in feet per second.
Suppose the range is 300 ft. What is the initial speed?

Completing the Unit Project

Now you are ready to write your math story. It should include these things.

- a setting, characters, and a plot
- at least three situations modeled by equations or formulas you studied earlier in this course
- at least one situation modeled by a baseball equation given in the "Working on the Unit Project" exercises
- at least one situation modeled by a soccer equation in the table on page 545

Look Back

Which form of the baseball and soccer path equations was most helpful in finding how far the ball traveled or how high it traveled? What difference did you find between the soccer equations when the ball was kicked and when it was struck with the head?

Assessing the Unit Project

4 points The math story is creative and appealing. It contains a setting, characters, and a plot incorporating situations using equations and formulas from previous units and from this unit. The equations chosen are appropriate models for the situations. The variables in the equations and formulas have reasonable values.

3 points The math story is acceptable but not particularly creative. The equations and formulas from this course have acceptable values for the variables.

2 points The math story is incomplete. It may not contain a setting, characters, or a plot. The situations modeled on equations and formulas from previous units in the course are incomplete. The situations modeled on the baseball and soccer equations are incomplete. The values for the variables in the equations and formulas are not reasonable. This story should be returned with suggestions for improvements and a new deadline.

1 point The story cannot be evaluated. It is illegible, incomplete, or not understandable. The story should be returned with a new deadline for completion. The group should be encouraged to speak with the teacher as soon as possible so that they understand the purpose and the format of the project.

Alternative Projects

Project 1: Mickey Mantle's Record Home Run

On May 22, 1963, Mickey Mantle hit a home run in Yankee Stadium that nearly went out of the park. This is reportedly the closest anyone has ever come to hitting an out-of-the-park home run in this stadium. Find out the details of this home run. Model the path of the ball with an equation and a graph. About how far from home plate would the ball have landed if it had not hit anything before it reached the ground?

Project 2: Making Parabolas from Straight Lines

Parabolas can be formed by straight lines. Research how this is done—
with paper folding, paper and pencil, or string. Then create a design that
contains at least three parabolas formed by straight lines.

Outside Resources

Burke, James. *Connections*, pp. 229–260. Toronto, Ontario, 1978. Video series is
also available from PBS.

Sportsworks. Toronto: Ontario Science Center, 1989.

The Physics of Sports. Optical Data's Science Multimedia Library, 1991.
(Macintosh)